The Anatomy of Tyrants

By

Mohamed F. El-Hewie

2011

TABLE OF CONTENTS

1. NAPOLEON BONAPARTE

Almost all tyrants took pride in the military uniform and extravagant appearance.
Napoleon Bonaparte knew of no boundaries for expansions, invasions and excessive use of force to execute his maniacal plans. His Egyptian expedition included a group of 167 scientists: mathematicians, naturalists, chemists and geodesists among them; their discoveries included the Rosetta Stone, and their work was published in the Description de l'Égypte in 1809. General Bonaparte conquered Cairo and executed its ruler, Omar Ebin El-Khatab.

After his futile invasion of the Egypt and Jerusalem, Bonaparte returned to France, declared himself Emperor and started recarving the boundaries of Europe. By 1812, his enemies grew stronger and were able to defeat Bonaparte, exile him to his death in 1815.

By 1804, England commissioned the first steam train, which was the first step towards powerful machines and mechanized industries. By 1830, England, again commissioned the electrical motor and the electrical age started in full gear.

Battle of the Pyramids, François-Louis-Joseph Watteau, 1798–1799. Napoleon executed the Omar Ebin El Khata, the governor of Cairo, which inflamed the Egyptians against his army and ended by the killing of his successor on the hands on an angry Syrian taking revenge for the massacres committed by Napoleon's army.

Bonaparte before the Sphinx, (ca. 1868) by Jean-Léon Gérôme, Hearst Castle. The Sphinx was safely buried under the sand in 1798 when the French invaded Egypt.

Bonaparte entered Al-Azhar Mosque, in Cairo, on the back of his horses, unaware of the grave consequences of his desecrating the most scared Islamic University in those days, 1798. Arial Sharon would repeat the same plunder in Jerusalem, Palestine by walking into the Islamic section of Al-Aqsa Mosque. As Bonaparte inflamed the entire Islamic World against France in 1798, Arial Sharon did the same in 1990's. Bonapart's desecration of Al-Azhar led to the Albanian and Otman soldier Muhammad Ali to travel to Egypt, eliminate the Mamlouk rulers, and govern and modernize Egypt until his death in 1840. Muhammad Ali gathered all the Arab rulers in the Citadel, in Cairo, and executed them all except one who escaped with his horse after jumping from a high cliff. Ali invaded Higaz (currently Saudi Arabia) and was the first invader in history who could have done so. Ali's grandsons would rule Egypt until 1952, before Naser carried out his revolution and expelled King Farouk from Egypt.

2. ADOLF HITLER

Adolf Hitler wore the military uniform in all occasions and relied on military power to execute maniacal invasions and destructions in the same route followed by Napoleon Bonaparte. In most of the world where Britain and France fought for colonial dominance, Hitler was cherished as hero who could break the back of the Great Britain and liberate its occupied subjects. Ghandi, in India, sought independence from Britain with peaceful means after the defeat of Hitler and weakening of Great Britain. In Palestine, King Abdulla was compelled to return to the British resolution of the Jewish Arab conflict of 1917 that promised the Jews a free state in Palestine. Even the USA refrained from entering WWII until it was attacked by Japan. Moreover, the USA dealt with Germany during its expansion of battles of the WWII.

Chronicle File

Killing Hitler required six years of brutal war and destruction. But, in 1945, Hitler was finally eliminated. Many of the Middle East Christians who named their kids after Adolph Hitler in hope for liberating the Jerusalem for the dominance of fanatic Jews, were now compelled to rename their kids differently. "Adolf" was changed to "Adeli" which became a common Arabic name for Christians and meant "wise man".

Daily Mirror

Wednesday, May 2, 1945
No. 12,800   ONE PENNY
Registered at G.P.O. as a Newspaper

"GERMANY WILL BATTLE ON"

HITLER DEAD

Killed in Berlin, says new Fuehrer, Admiral Doenitz

Adolf Hitler, leader of the Nazi Party since January 20, 1933, who passed a death-defeated man, dead at the age of fifty-six.

HITLER was killed in action yesterday afternoon, according to a broadcast from Hamburg at 10.30 last night.

His successor is Rear-Admiral Doenitz, the C-in-C. of the German Navy, who made the announcement himself.

Doenitz said: "The Fuehrer has fallen at his command post in Berlin. He fell for Germany."

This is Doenitz

"MY FIRST TASK," SAID DOE-NITZ, "IS TO SAVE THE GERMAN PEOPLE FROM DESTRUCTION BY BOL-SHEVISM. IT ONLY FOR THIS TASK THE STRUGGLE WILL CONTINUE."

"Give me your obedience. Do your daily. Keep order. Only in this way shall we be able to prevent collapse.

The German newspaper must close before the flames of destruction rage.

After a lull at dawn, Hamburg radio said:

"It is reported today the Fuehrer's headquarters that our Fuehrer Adolf Hitler has fallen this afternoon in his Berlin Chancery, still fighting to the last breath against Bolshevism and for Germany.

"On April 30 the Fuehrer appointed Grand Admiral Doenitz as his successor.

"Our new Fuehrer will speak to the German people."

This new statement will probably be made today.

Continued on Back Page

'Lay down your arms' —Graziani to his Army

Marshal Graziani, commander of the armies of Marshal Kesselring, has ordered all the German and Italian troops under his command to lay down their arms.

'Wait' is Churchill's tip to the Commons

M r. Churchill, in the House of Commons yesterday, warned members not to be surprised if no immediate official confirmation of the news came through.

"This news came Fuehrer has spoken for the German people.

Continued on Back Page

DANES ARE TAKING OVER FROM THE GERMAN ARMY

CIVIL SERVANTS ARE ASKING FOR HIGHER PAY

Snowfire
BEAUTY MAKERS
For sure and clean

Hitler's facial apathy is characteristic of schizophrenia. His paranoid delusions narrow such diagnosis to paranoid schizophrenia.

Hitler's facial expressions conveyed anger and resentment in every photo taken for him. But this painting attempted to lighten his gloomy apathy.

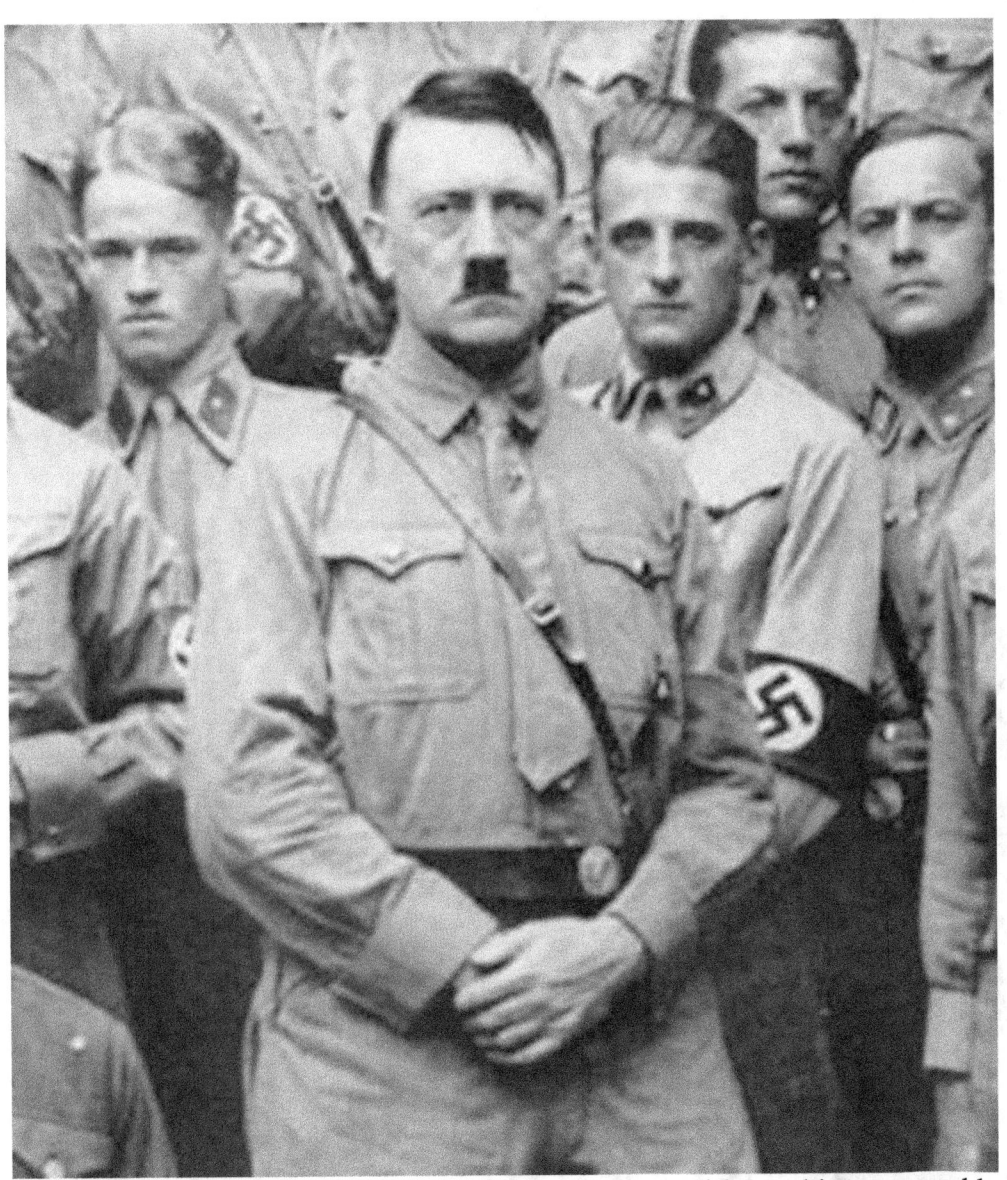

Comparing the facial expressions of those around Hitler to his, one could easily discern the gloom and doom with the man's dark inside.

Neville Chamberlain and Adolf Hitler
September 1939

Hitler's tense facial expressions are enforced by his arm grabbing, compared to the docile demeanor of Neville Chamberlain, the Prime Minster of Britain.

The extravagant military appearance suffices to show the threat of unrestrained Nazism and Fascism prior to WWII.

Hitler lived in the age of wireless communication and powerful electrical and gasoline driven engines. Yet, none of the modern advances of technology lent him any greater advantage over Bonaparte. Both died killed, defeated, and defamed. Both, Bonaparte and Hitler aimed far beyond the imaginable reaches of their people and resources and angered millions of opponents and followers. Indeed, both tyrants were equally suicidal as the rest of tyrants described in this book.

3. JOSEPH STALIN

Joseph Stalin did not differ from Hitler or Napoleon in his extravagant outlook or fierce reliance of force to crush his opponents. However, Stalin differed from the two tyrants in his pleasant facial expressions and his refrain from invasion of other territories unless he was provoked.

British Prime Minister Winston Churchill, President Franklin Roosevelt and Soviet Premier Joseph Stalin in Russian Crimea (now Ukraine) at the 1945 Yalta Conference, where the leaders discussed post-World War II organization of Europe. Even in a civilian meting, Stalin wore his military uniform, as style that was followed by Qaddafi, Sadat, and Castro.

Stalin's brutal elimination of his internal opponents differed from Hitler's hatred toward folks of non Aryan races.

Even in his youth, Stalin had attractive and pleasant look compared to the apathy and gloom of Hitler.

The aging tyrant has eliminated not only his opponents, but also his closest family members.

At old age, Stalin lost his ability to cheer, his cigarette never left his drooping and shaky fingers.

Stalin's death saddens millions who cherished his brutal elimination of dissenting voices and brought order to a chaotic empire.

Whether the grief of the death of Stalin was true emotional loss or disbelief in the fact that tyrants die like the rest of us? Stalin's corpse in the coffin still carries his fierce soul that dominated Russia for 35 years.

Stalin finally rested in peace while millions of his victims were deprived of such human dignity.

Dead but not forgotten and is still even adored by the old generation of Russia who viewed Stalin as a man of steel will and unshakable principles.

4. MUAMMAR QADDAFI

Qaddafi was totally wasted in almost all his documented public appearances. But here, in Rome, his old enemy and occupier, Qaddafi invokes resentment in his audience with bizarre appearance and incoherent and irrelevant talk.

Barak Obama was too naïve to shake hand with a deranged tyrant.

In Rome, Qaddafi still wears his military uniform, covers his intoxicated eyes, and expresses gloomy and inexplicable anger.

Qaddafi is the only head of an Arab state that employs women as his security guards.

Totally intoxicated, wearing eccentric and extravagant military uniform, Qaddafi ruled
Libya for 42 years, since his military coup in 1969. Like all military dictators, Qaddafi
never engaged in two-way public dialogues where he could explain his inebriated
outlook.

Qaddafi's irresistible and spontaneous anger could not been explained other than by his own statement advising the youth to stay late at night, never sleep, sing and dance.

Libya fought Italy for liberation from European colonialism, yet to fall under the reign of Qaddafi. Qaddafi overthrow King Idris by the help of Naser and relied on Naser's wide appeal in the Arab World in order to numb his people towards his inapt leadership.

The old Soviet Union is gone, but Qaddafi is still grateful to the Russians for arming him from ground up. This is the first photo that shows Qaddafi's pleasant demeanor and would not be repeated often. This is also the only photo that shows the proper facial reaction that suits the occasion since Russia was the main life support of Qaddafi, Naser, Castro, and Saddam.

The African dream of strong leader in Libya has been waiting for 42 years, while Qaddafi wasted into unhealthy life style. Arriving to power at the age of 29, Qaddafi has no education beyond the high school when the Libyan schools lacked all standards of basic education. In reality, Qaddafi was totally illiterate despite his high military status as King Idris lacked the man power to rule Libya. Thus, Qaddafi's eccentric behaviors are closely related to his total lack of education, life experience and his access the enormous resources of an oil wealthy state.

Even in this eccentric civilian suite, Qaddafi still wears the military badges for no apparent purpose other than his apparent detachment.

The combination of outlandish military uniform, unkempt hair, were always combined with this angry facial expressions.

Qaddafi's attack on the UN mimics Nikita Khrushchev and Naser's speech to the same body. Qaddafi has slipped in time and froze into his 1969's days of his military coup.

What causes the man to portray such repulsive outlook?

Saif Al-Islam or the Sword of Islam is Qaddafi's son. His Western education made him more reasonable than Kim Jong's son of the North Korea. But, Saif Al-Islam waited until his father sunk into the deep hole of public unrest and rejection.

Qaddafi's irresponsible lifestyle was impossible to conceal in every photo taken for him. His loneliness and remoteness reflected on his gloomy outlook.

The irrelevance of Qaddafi's outlandish military outfit to the occasion of meeting with the Prime Minster of Italy might be reconciled with the past animosity between Italy and Libya.

Qaddafi's covered every spot of his outfit with colorful decoration in total contrast to his gloomy appearance that is hidden behind his sun glasses and head cover.

In a continent stricken by poverty and disease, cultural taboos stand in the way of opening to the outside world.

Can Qaddafi truly read?
All signs of schizophrenia are demonstrated in his appearance: apathy, indifference, unkempt appearance, and bizarre thoughts.

Early during his youth, Qaddafi showed leaner body and much better personal care than his latter years. Here, his military outfit, though outlandish, is still much soothing than his maniacal dressing in his latter years.

.

Qaddafi's choice of improper colors is one among many of his eccentric behaviors.

Totally wasted, Qaddafi gives kisses to his admirers.

With apparent liver failure, the man might also suffer from impaired judgment due to the same malady. Even with the standards of the Middle East, such appearance belongs to homeless or stray people.

The typical feature of hypothyroidism of dull facial appearance may also be complicated with his shot liver and poor lifestyle.

Still holds to the stick from the era of living nomad when the stick was the only weapon a man could devise with least of troubles.

On one side, Qaddafi has no single human being in his vicinity, no second opinion to be shared. On the other side, the masses were not allowed to question his ultimate rules of governing their republic.

.

King Muhammed Idris under estimated the menace of empowering illiterate youth to the highest military ranks. He would be thrown out of his crown and Libya would fall under the reign of an inebriated young officer: Muaammar Qaddafi.

That was all that Qaddafi earned: Military uniform is a tribal nation that could not afford to offer basic elementary education to its pupils.

It was not enough to decorate his military uniform with such extravagant items, so Qaddafi opted to attach photographs on his uniform.

Even though Libya could afford to provide air-conditioning to its ruler, Qaddafi still stinks under heavy layers of cloths. His hypothyroidism might explain his intolerance to cold and his dull facial outlook.

Covered from head to toes, Qaddafi still could not hide his bizarre facial outlook from the small portion exposed of his face.

Qaddafi and the flowers, in an empty setting except of a sick man with edematous face and deep seated misery.

5. FIDEL CASTRO

Fidel Castro shared the same angry outlook, wore his military uniform, and was forced to retire only after crippling illness.

Castro also engaged in no dialogue. He was the only one to talk and no talk back was allowed.

Carter's probing into the minds of evil dictators stemmed from deep religious conviction. But, Castro was unshakable in his long delusion of power and control.

Only Carter could do that after leaving the office.

6. SADDAM HUSSEIN

The paranoia of power blinded Saddam from such fate of being cornered into a ditch in his old village.

Could he really read what he holds in his hand?

Cleaned up for execution, Saddam made a new historic landmark in the unforeseen moral connection between the three eastern religions. A brutal Muslim dictator was brought to ultimate justice on the hands on a Christian army that saved the fate of millions of Muslims ruled by such despot.

"God Is Great" was attached to the Iraqi flag after the 8 year war with Iran. Every thing Stalin presented, except of Stalin's pleasant outlook, Saddam appeared in his military uniform, expressing anger on his immediate supporters. Those would soon turn him in to the American invaders to be executed.

Saddam posing as soldier which he has never been one.

A historic moment in the marsh of Christianity to deliver justice to the cruelest place on earth: Iraq.

George Bush inapt presentation deprived him from earning credit for the greatest achievement of bringing justice to Saddam.

7. ARIAL SHARON

Arial Sharon had unlimited access to the White House due to the Jewish voters and the Zionist lobby that monopolized the American government. Sharon defied all American ideals of equality, liberty, and the pursuit of happiness. His death with stroke has never been publicized. He made sure to poison Arafat prior to Sharon's falling into irreversible coma. Both Arafat and Sharon departed in proximate dates.

The highest Israeli military ranks were given to every maniac who believes in cleansing the Arabs from Palestine and replacing them by Jews. Sharon earned it fair and square.

8. HOSNI MUBARAK

Military assassination has always been the only mean of changing the Egyptian government. With the total absence of democracy, bullets did the talk. This is the scene that preceded the assassination of Anwar Sadat.

Mubarak, Sadat, and Gazala were the top military leaders in Egypt on October 6, 1981 when Sadat was shot.

After 30 years rule under emergency law, Mubarak still believed that he could hang to power from February, 2011 till September 2011. Few hours later, he vanished without a trace.

9. KIM JONG

Kim Jong Ill turned North Korea into isolated, impoverished nation with his maniacal delusions. Kim Jong shared the features of dictators of wearing military uniform, not engaging in dialogue with his people, and expressive apathy towards the aspiration of the nation.

The son of Kim Jong Ill knows nothing different from his father's obsession with power and control.

From behind concrete barrier and with elderly and closed relatives, the son of Jong Ill commences his father's legacy.

The military rule is very common among all dictators without the slightest exception and Kim Jong is no different.

The father and the son high and large above all.

10. SLOBODAN MILOŠEVIĆ

Slobodan Milošević expressed resentment as Jesse Jackson improvises this casual photo opportunity. Slobodan Milošević was already cornered and nearing defeat as the American bombing was ongoing, strangulating Serbia from Kosovo.

Slobodan Milošević never appeared in military uniform but employed the military to do his dirty work.

In the Balkans, the bull horn sufficed to ignite WWI and did the same for Slobodan Milošević.

Slobodan Milošević replicated the role of Arial Sharon but was crushed by the Western powers due to the sensitive location of Serbia in the heart of prospering Europe.

Kosovo's genocide gathered enough anger that moved the world against Slobodan Milošević.

For some, Slobodan Milošević was a patriot and a hero.

Bin Laden shared all features of tyrants except the state. Thus, Bin Laden resorted to the lawless state of Afghanistan where he could execute the same plots that occupied napoleon, Hitler, Stalin, Saddam, -Qaddafi, Sharon, and Castro. Bin Laden relied on violence, engaged in one sided speeches, and stayed the course with relentless determination.

In an impoverished Islamic countries, where corruption and greed ran amok, Bin Laden offered the spirit of Omar Bin Khatab, the third Khaliffa who expnaded Muhammad's mission from Mecca and Medina in Saudi Arabia, to Spain in Europe and Philippine in the far east of Asia. Bin laden docile personality and coherent reasoning appealed to many poorly educated and young men and women. Bin Laden strengthened his Base with his swift and persistent actions.

For many experienced and young adults, Bin Laden represented an entertaining character bent on destruction and upheaval with no realistic strategies to attend to real life demands.

CONCLUSION

All tyrants shared the following characteristics:

1. **Never engaged in dialogues** or efforts to present their purposes, motivations, or the means to achieve their goals.
2. All relied on **power and violence** to execute their plans.
3. All came from either **illiterate upbringing or radical religious** indoctrination.
4. Most expressed direct and apparent **apathy and bizarre and eccentric behavior.**
5. All were **men, single, and isolated.**
6. All were removed from power either by **death, assassination, or escape** from prosecution.
7. All tyrants raised **old conflicts** to highest level of attention that required international effort to resolve.
8. All aimed to **greater theatres** to reach their audiences than their immediate territory.
9. All used **flags, specific attire** to display their specific class.